RECORDED VERSIONS
GUITAR ®

AUTHENTIC TRANSCRIPTIONS
WITH NOTES AND TABLATURE

D1215464

**Music transcriptions by
Jeff Jacobson and Colin Higgins**

ISBN 0-634-02122-2

HAL•LEONARD®
CORPORATION

7777 W. BLUEMOUND RD. P.O. BOX 13819 MILWAUKEE, WI 53213

Visit Hal Leonard Online at
www.halleonard.com

available on Atlantic Records.   Management: Michael Lippman / LIPPMAN ENTERTAINMENT Produced by **Matt Serletic** for Melisma Productions, Inc. Recorded by Noel Golde

ring by Mark Dobson Mixed by David Thoener Art Direction and Design: Ria Lewerke, Paul Doucette, Imagic   Cover Art: Michael Sowa Photography: Dean Karr except pages 2 & 3 Andrew Macpherson, pages 4 & 5 by James Minchin III

adam gaynor

brian yale

kyle cook

season

rob thomas

paul doucette

boxtwenty

www.matchboxtwenty.com

Angry

Written by Rob Thomas

Gtr. 6; Drop D tuning:
(low to high) D–A–D–G–B–E

Intro
Moderately Rock ♩ = 120

* Vol. swell

* Refers to bkgd. vocs. only

11

Chorus

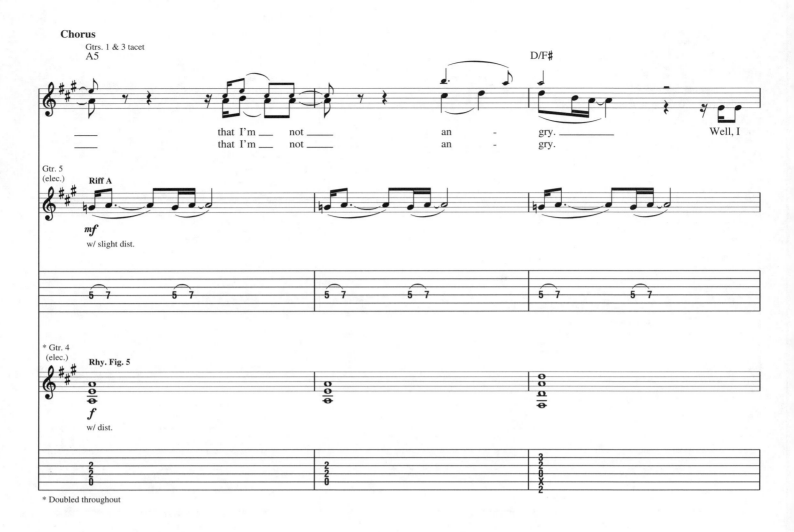

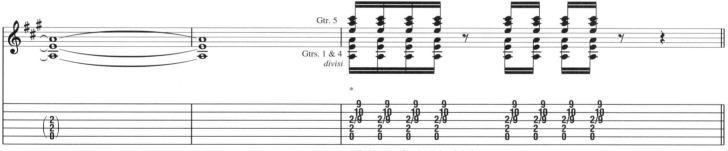

* Gtr. 5 notated to the right of slash.

Verse
Gtr. 1: w/ Rhy. Fig. 2 (2 times)
Gtr. 4 tacet

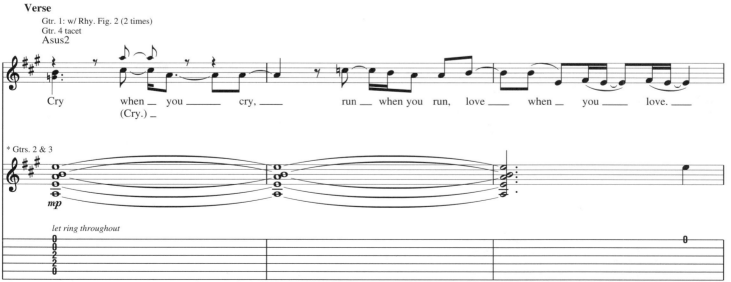

* Composite arrangement

- gry and I've nev-er been a - bove ___ it. You ___ see through ___ me, don't ___ you?_____ Yeah._

Guitar Solo

Gtr. 6 tacet

Gtr. 7 (elec.)

f
w/ dist.
let ring throughout

Gtr. 8 (elec.)

f
w/ slight dist.

grad. bend

Gtr. 4

It's good

grad. bend

Chorus

Gtr. 4: w/ Rhy. Fig. 5 (2 times)
Gtr. 5: w/ Riff A (2 times)
Gtrs. 7 & 8 tacet

that I'm   not   an - gry.   Well, I   need   to   get   o - ver. And I'm,
(...that I'm   not   an - gry.

Voc. Fig. 3

End Voc. Fig. 3

(I'm   not   an - gry.   I'm   not...)

Bkgd. Voc.: w/ Voc. Fig. 3 (3 times)

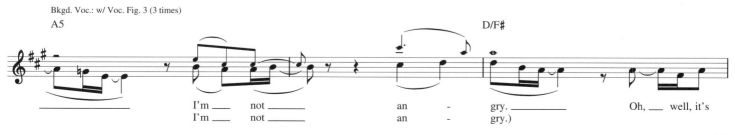

I'm   not   an - gry.   Oh,   well, it's
I'm   not   an - gry.)

Black & White People

Written by Rob Thomas

Verse

Gtrs. 1, 2 & 4 tacet

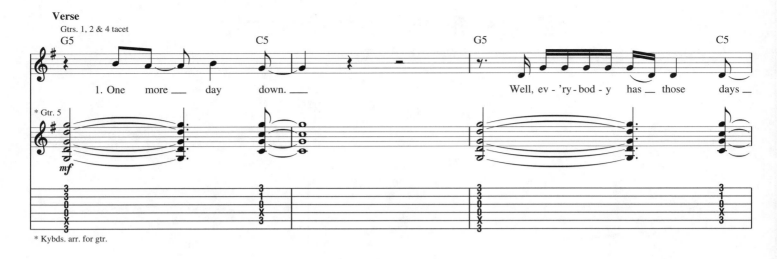

* Kybds. arr. for gtr.

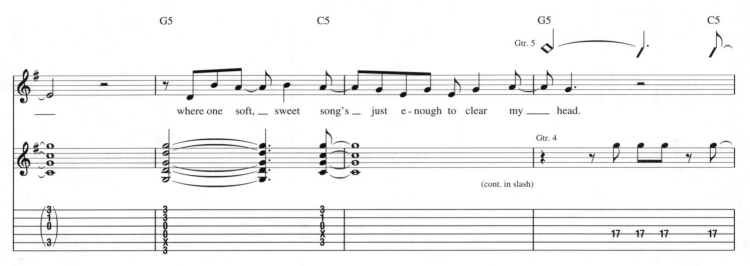

(cont. in slash)

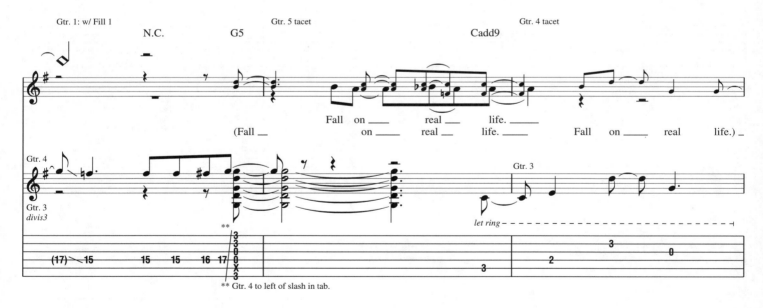

** Gtr. 4 to left of slash in tab.

Tech - ni - col - or dreams.   of black and white peo - ple.

Verse

Gtrs. 1, 2, 4 & 6 tacet

2. One boy, head - strong, he thinks that liv - ing here's just plain.

He's pushed down so hard you can hear him start to sink.

And it's one last round

Gtr. 3: w/ Rhy. Fill 1

Cadd9

Tech - ni - col - or dreams _____ of black and white peo -

8va
End Fill 2

Interlude

Gtr. 7 tacet

A5   G E5   Cadd9   B A5

⑥ 3fr   ⑤ 2fr

Gtrs. 1 & 2

- ple.

Gtr. 4

G E5   D5

⑥ 3fr

Rhy. Fill 1
Gtr. 3

let ring ----------

25

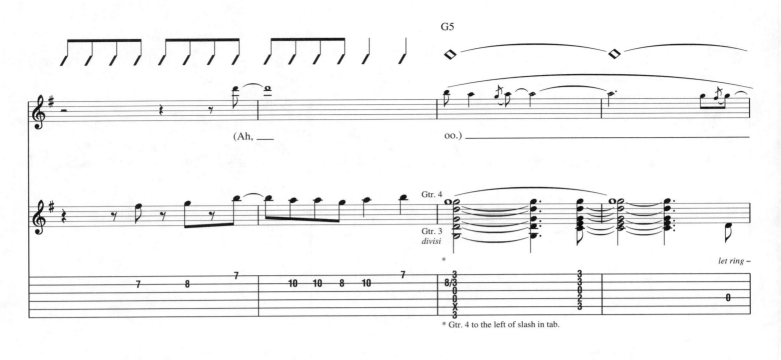

* Gtr. 4 to the left of slash in tab.

Verse

Gtrs. 1 & 2 tacet

Gtr. 4 tacet

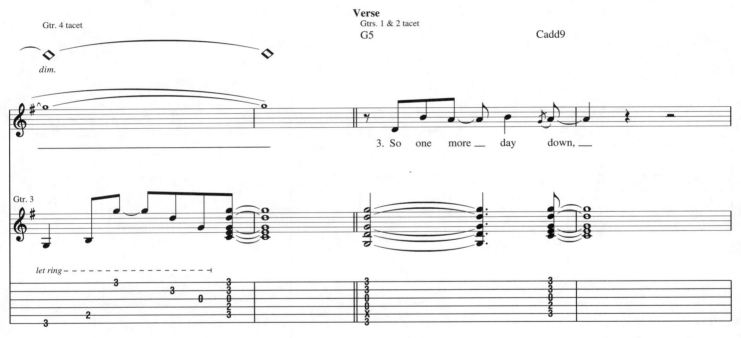

3. So one more __ day down, __

and ev-'ry-bod-y's chang - in'.

One soft, __ sweet sound's __ just e - nough to clear my, __

Chorus
2nd time, Gtrs. 1 & 3: w/ Rhy. Fill 2
Gtr. 2: w/ Rhy. Fig. 1A (1st 6 meas.)

my head. _____ And if it's just that you're weak, _ can we talk _ a - bout _ it?
ple. Hell, _ if you're weak, _

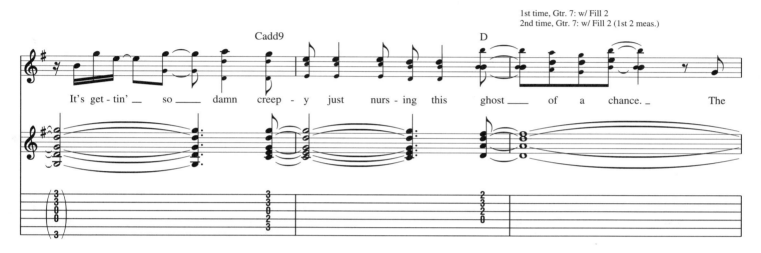

1st time, Gtr. 7: w/ Fill 2
2nd time, Gtr. 7: w/ Fill 2 (1st 2 meas.)

It's get - tin' _ so _ damn creep - y just nurs - ing this ghost ___ of a chance. _ The

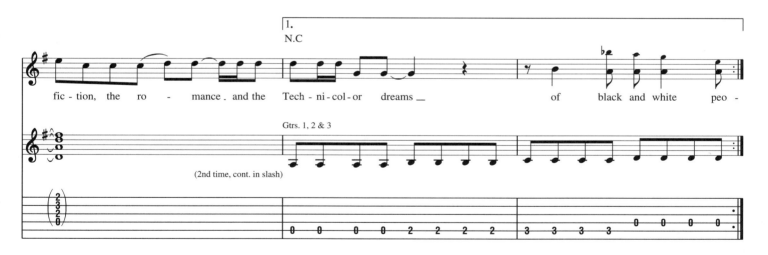

fic - tion, the ro - mance _ and the Tech - ni - col - or dreams ___ of black and white peo -

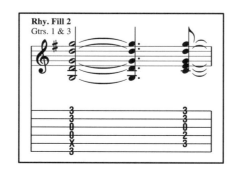

27

Tech - ni - col - or dreams _ of black and white peo - ple.

We are black and white. Yeah, ___ we are black and white peo -

ple. Yeah, ___ we are black and white peo - ple.

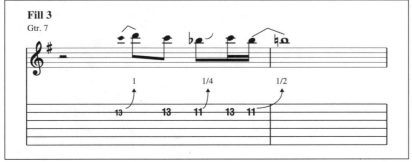

Fill 3
Gtr. 7

Crutch

Written by Rob Thomas

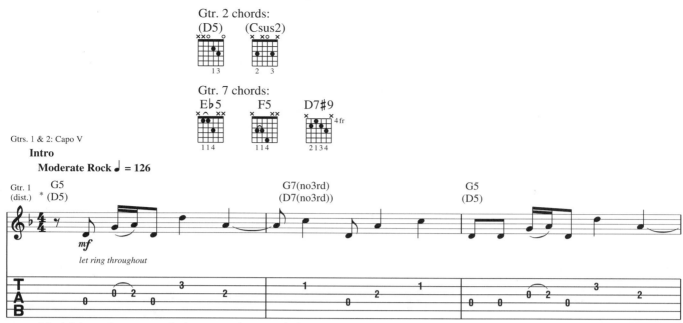

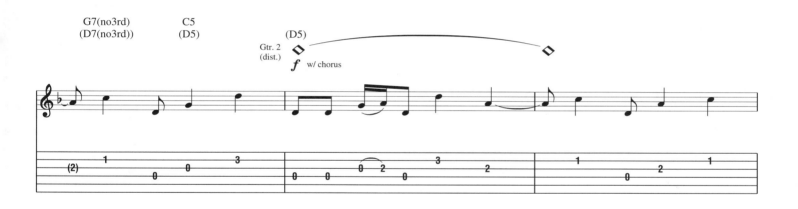

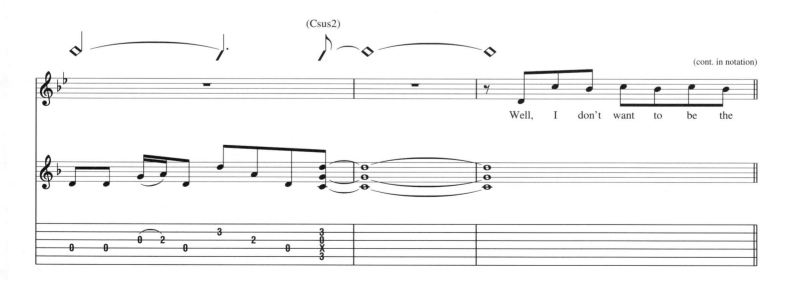

Verse

Gtrs. 1-4 tacet

N.C.(Gm)

1. Man, I feel __ like hell, __ so come on o - ver, be a love ma - chine __ and I could be your friend. __

Ain't no shame, __ feel strong __ for one an - oth - er. Make a real true col - or come end to end, __ then, __

Cm9

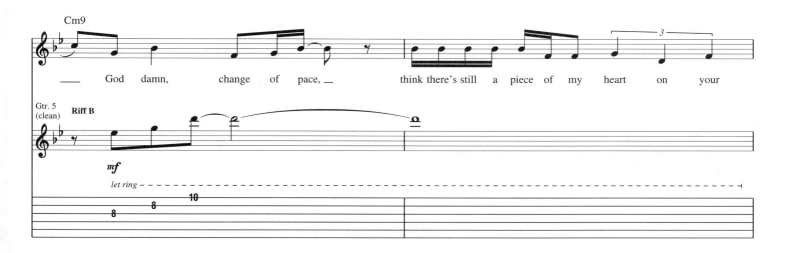

__ God damn, change of pace, __ think there's still a piece of my heart on your

Gtr. 5
(clean)

Riff B

mf

let ring -

```
10
    8
  8
```

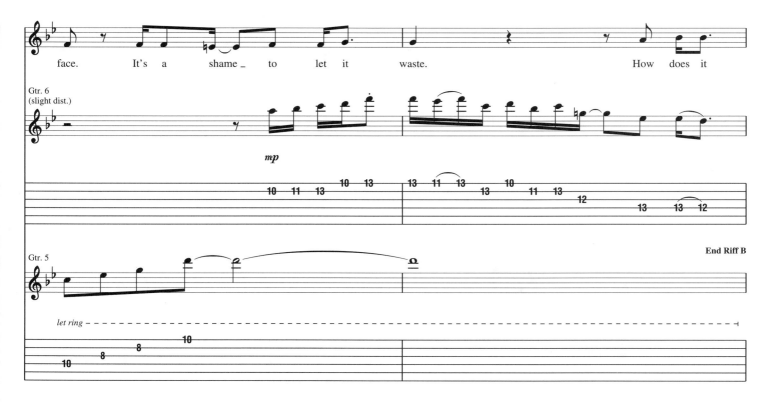

face. It's a shame __ to let it waste. How does it

Gtr. 6
(slight dist.)

mp

```
                    10  13   13 11 13   10
        10 11 13                  13      11  13
                                           12
                                      13  13  12
```

Gtr. 5

End Riff B

let ring -

```
        10
    8  8
10
```

31

32

Verse

3. Bring it on, ___ then gone __ and use a lov - er like a cig - a - rette __ the way that lov - ers do. __ One

__ sweet song __ that starts __ a lit - tle slow and then goes on __ and on __ and makes __ you want __ to

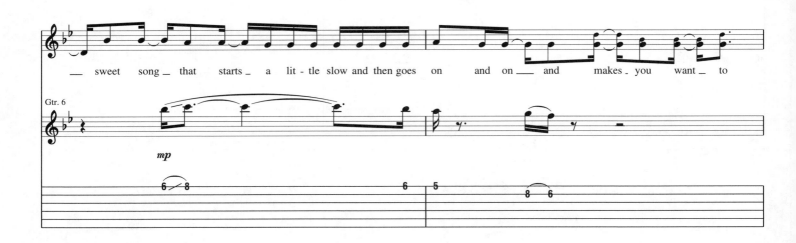

Gtr. 5: w/ Riff B (1 1/2 times)

Cm9

move a - round __ the room __ in cir - cles. Ev - 'ry bod - y wants... .
(Ev - 'ry bod - y wants __ to be you.) __

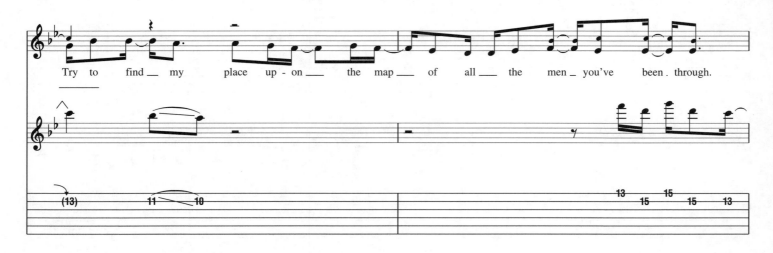

Try to find __ my place up - on __ the map __ of all __ the men __ you've been . through.

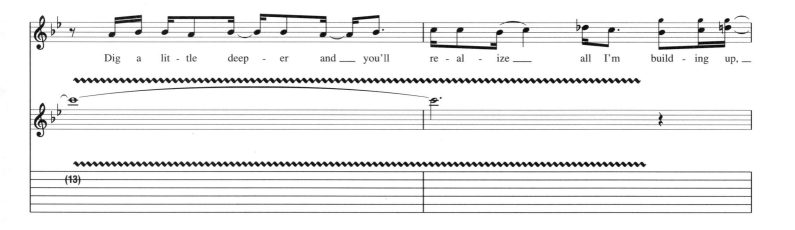

Dig a lit-tle deep - er and __ you'll re-al-ize __ all I'm build - ing up, __

D.S. al Coda 1

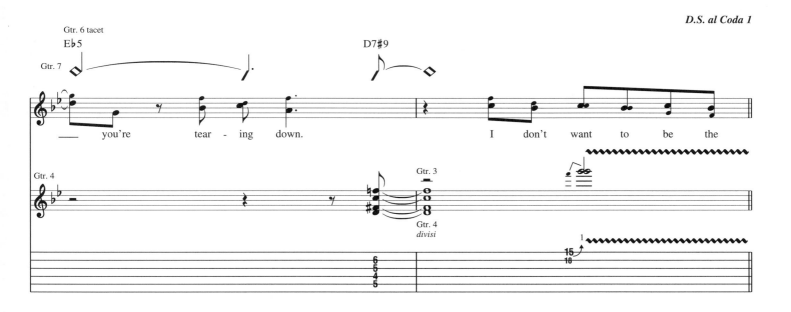

__ you're tear - ing down. I don't want to be the

⊕ Coda 1

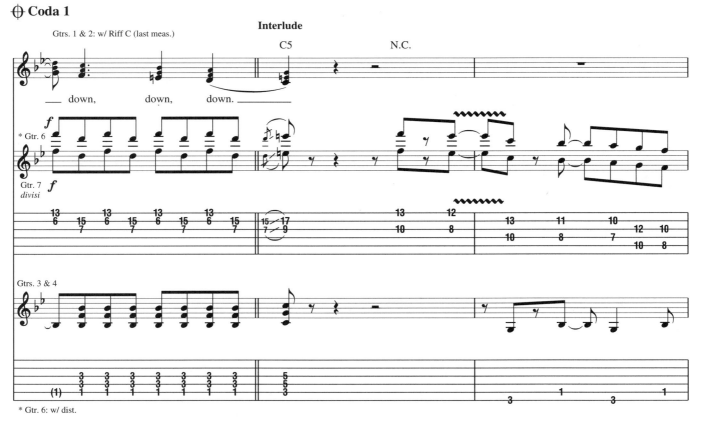

down, down, down. __

* Gtr. 6: w/ dist.

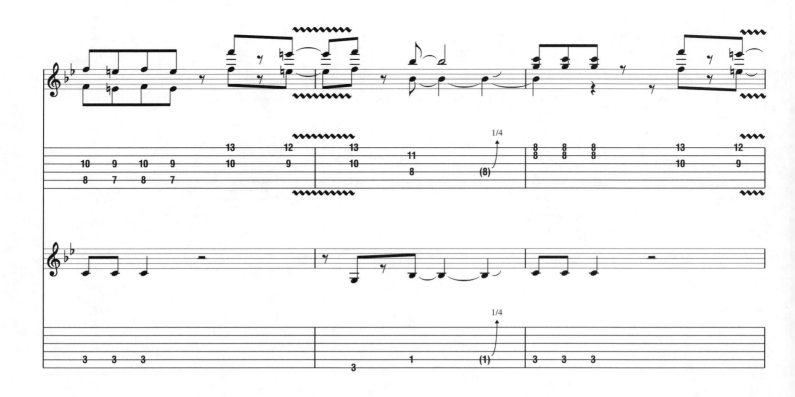

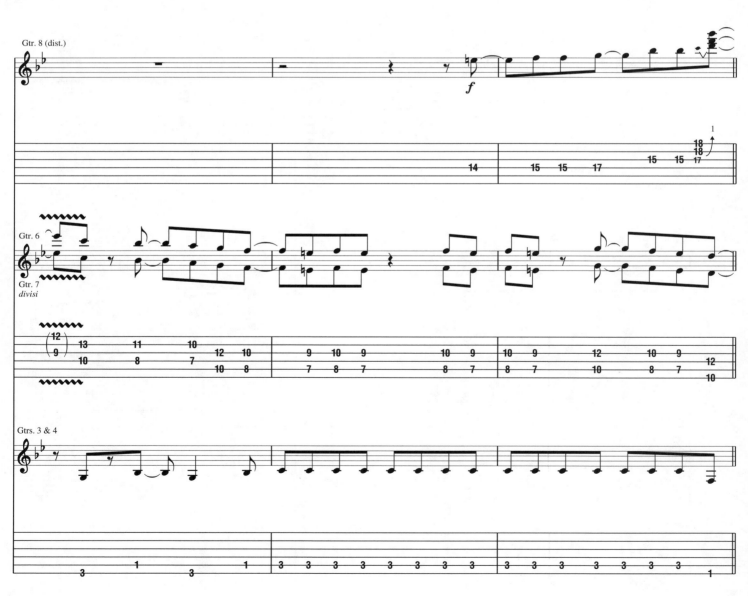

Guitar Solo

Gtrs. 6 & 7: w/ Fill 1

Last Beautiful Girl

Written by Rob Thomas and Matt Serletic

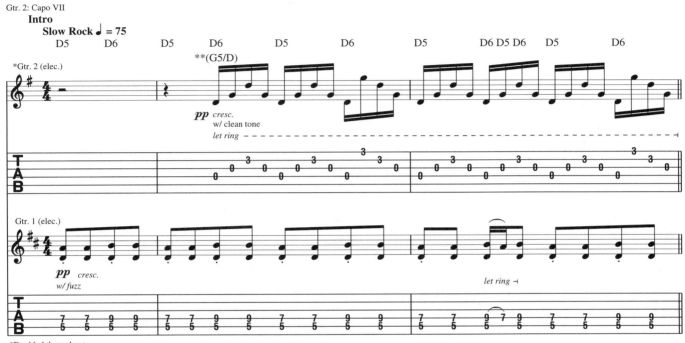

Gtr. 2: Capo VII

Intro
Slow Rock ♩ = 75

*Gtr. 2 (elec.)

*Doubled throughout

**Symbols in parentheses represent chord names respective to capoed gtr.
Symbols above reflect actual sounding chord. Capoed fret is "0" in tab.

Verse

Gtr. 1 tacet

1. This will all _____ fall down, _ like ev-'ry-thing else _ that was. _

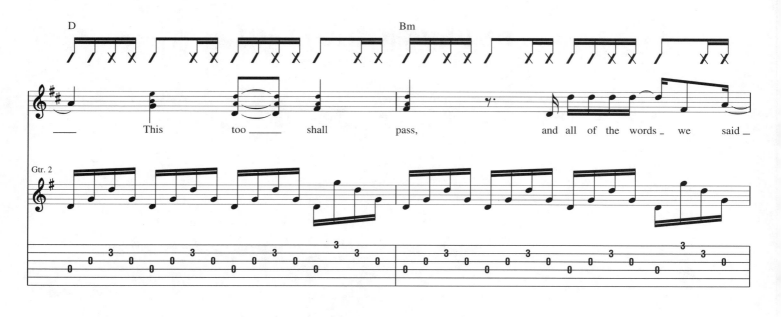

D   Bm

This too ___ shall pass, and all of the words ___ we said ___

Gtr. 2

Em   A   G5   **End Rhy. Fig. 1**

we can't take ___ back.   2. Now, ___

End Rhy. Fig. 1A

Verse
Gtrs. 2 & 3: w/ Rhy. Figs. 1 & 1A

D   Bm   D
(G)   (Em)   (G)

ev - 'ry fool ___ in ___ town   would - 've left ___ by now. ___ I can't re -
tell me one ___ more ___ time   how you're sor - ry a-bout ___ the way ___ this all went ___

Bm   Em
(Em)   (Am)

place   all of the wast - ed days, ___   the mem - o - ry of ___ your face. ___
down.   You need - ed to find ___ your space, ___   you need - ed to still ___ be friends. ___

Gtr. 1

40

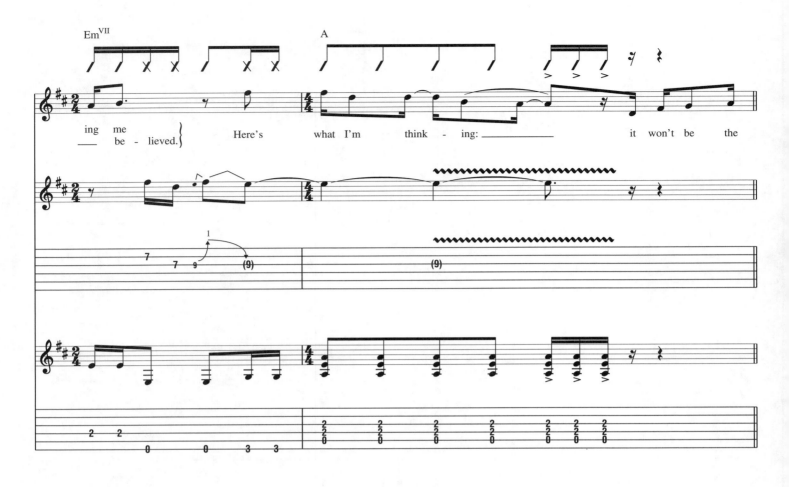

Chorus

Gtrs. 1, 4 & 5 tacet

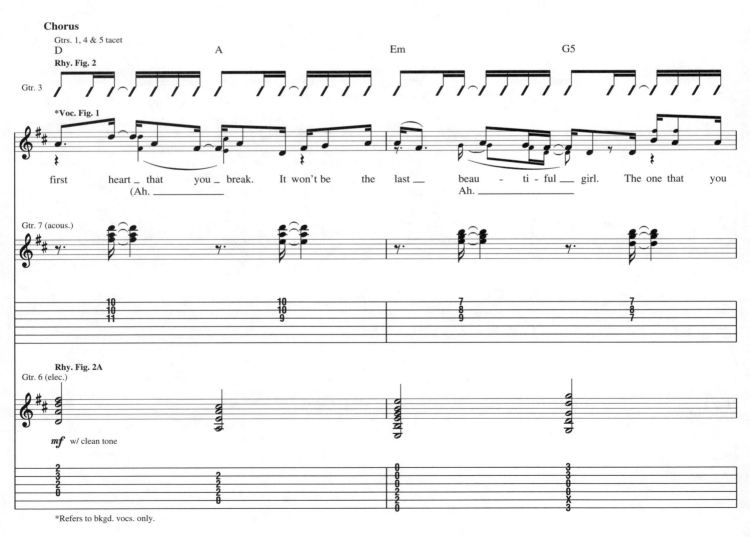

*Refers to bkgd. vocs. only.

If You're Gone

Written by Rob Thomas

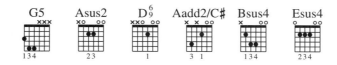

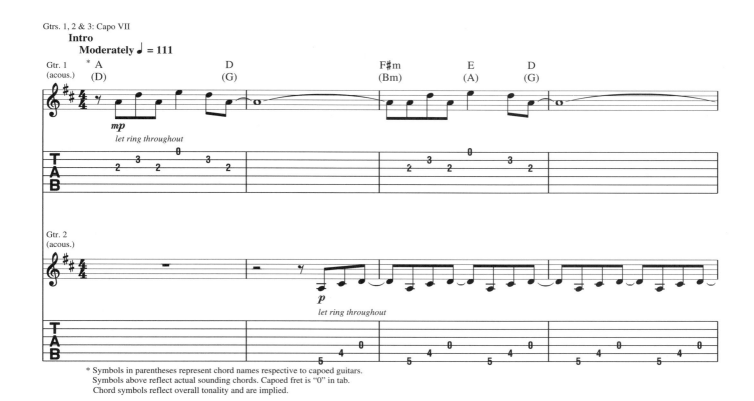

* Symbols in parentheses represent chord names respective to capoed guitars.
  Symbols above reflect actual sounding chords. Capoed fret is "0" in tab.
  Chord symbols reflect overall tonality and are implied.

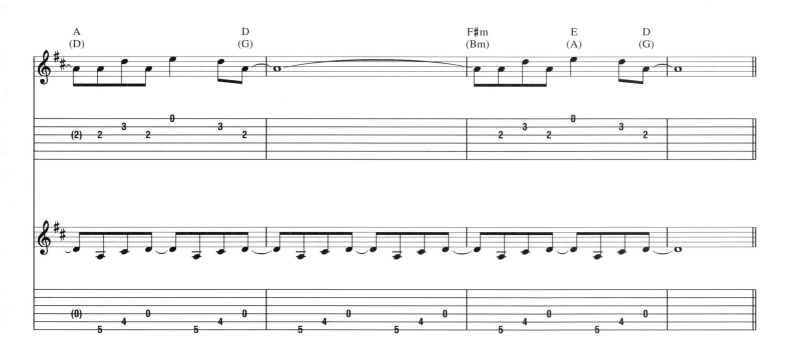

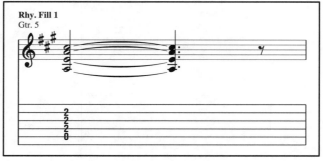

in ev - 'ry-thing in, ___ in ___ you. ___

* Horns arr. for gtr.

I think you're so mean, ___ I think we should try. ___ I think I could need ___

___ this in my life ___ and I think I'm scared. Do I ___ talk too ___

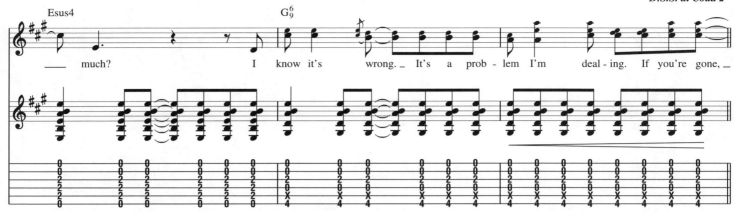

⊕ Coda 2

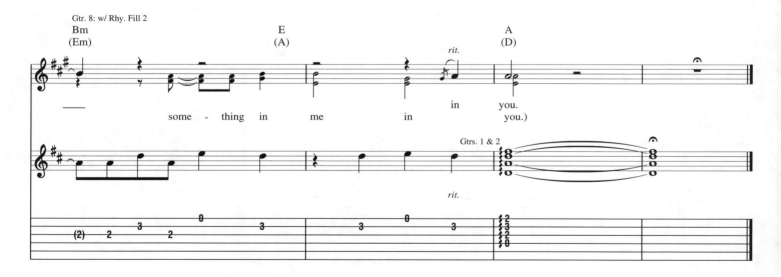

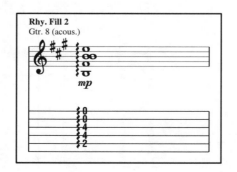

Mad Season

Written by Rob Thomas

Gtrs. 4 & 5: Capo III
Gtr. 9: Capo I

Intro

Moderately slow Rock ♩ = 86

*Kybd. arr. for gtr.

**Symbols in parentheses represent chord names respective to capoed gtr.
Symbols above reflect actual sounding chord. Capoed fret is "0" in tab.

54

So why ya got - ta stand __ there __ look - ing like the an - swer now? __
So are you gon - na stand __ there? __ Are you gon - na help me out? __

It seems to me __ you'd come a - round.
We need to be __ to - geth - er now.

I need you now. __

*Gtr. 6 (dist.)

Riff B

*Doubled throughout

**Chord symbols reflect basic harmony.

grad. bend 1/2

End Riff B

Fill 2
Gtr. 3

Interlude

Gtr. 1: w/ Riff A (2 times)
Gtr. 3: w/ Rhy. Fig. 1 (1 1/2 times)
Gtr. 4: w/ Rhy. Fig. 1A (2 times)
Gtrs. 7 & 8 tacet

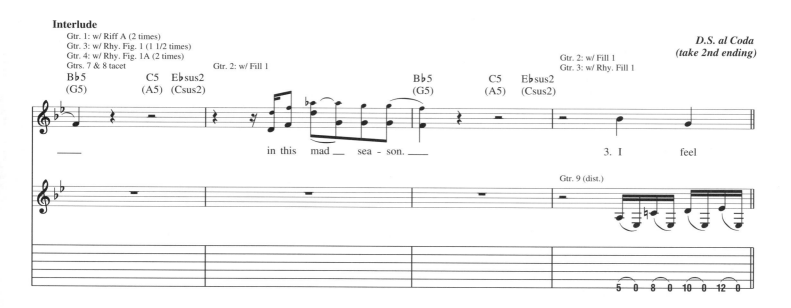

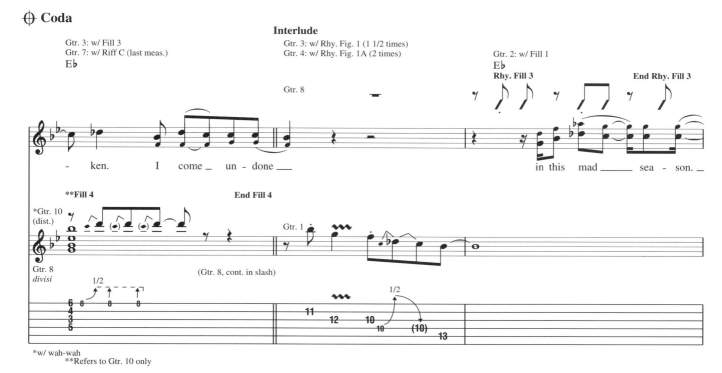

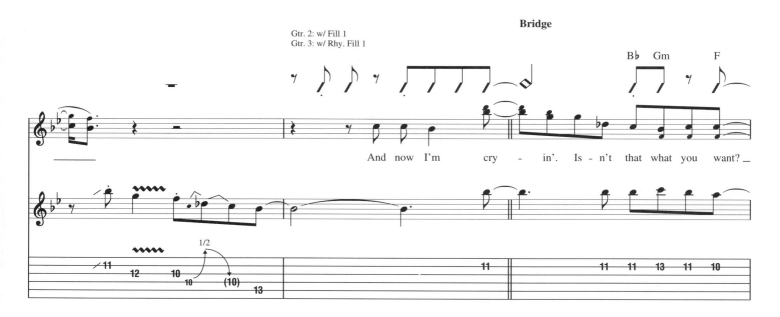

*w/ wah-wah
**Refers to Gtr. 10 only

And I'm try-in' __ to live my life on my own, __ but I won't, __ no. At times __
(What you want __ and I'm try-in'.)

*Bkgd. voc. doubled an octave higher.

__ I do be-lieve I am strong, __ so some-one tell me why, why, __ why __

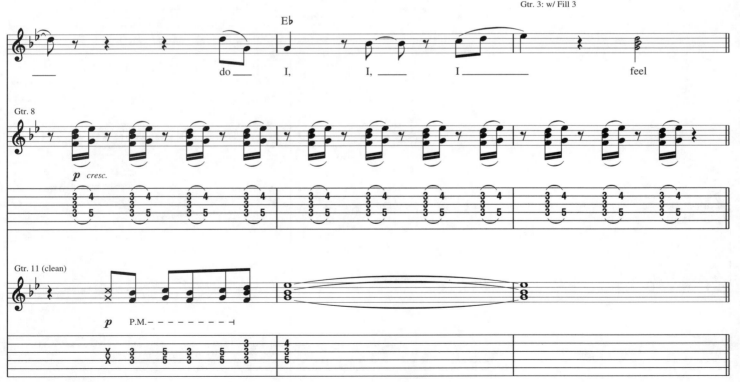

__ do __ I, I, __ I __ feel

Interlude

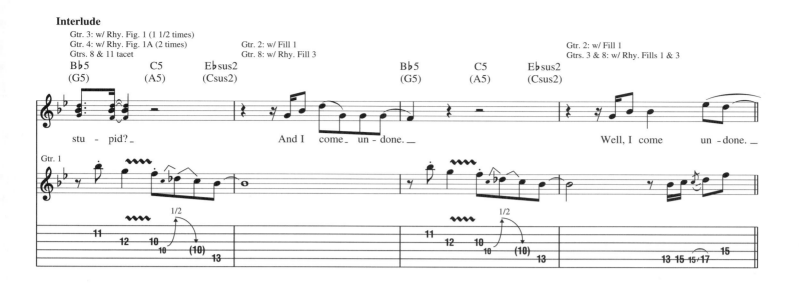

Guitar Solo

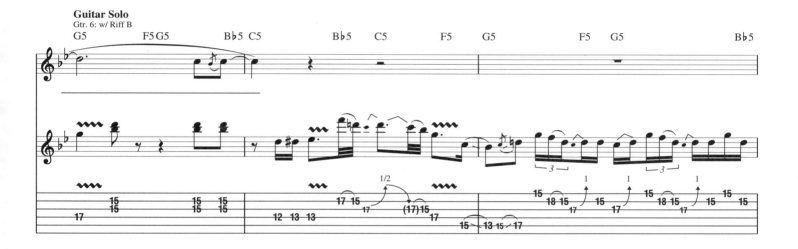

Chorus

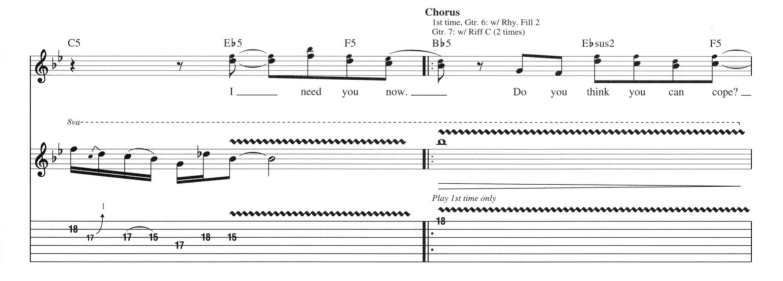

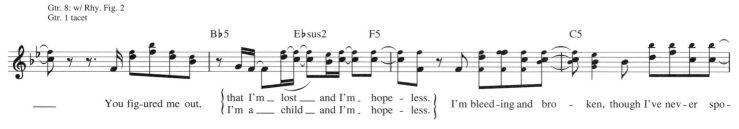

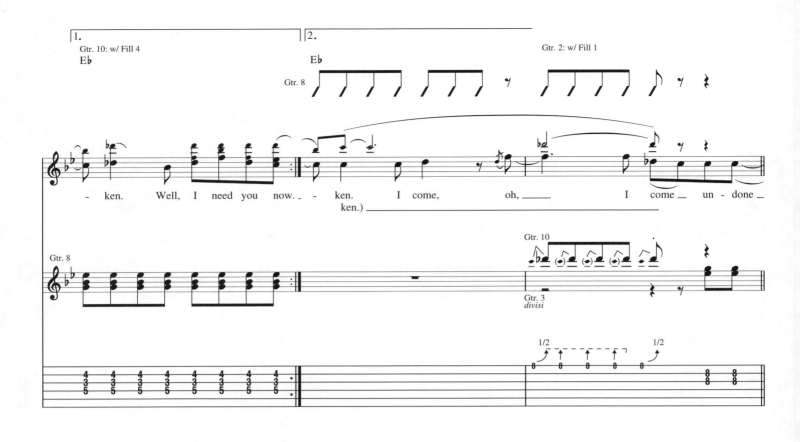

Outro

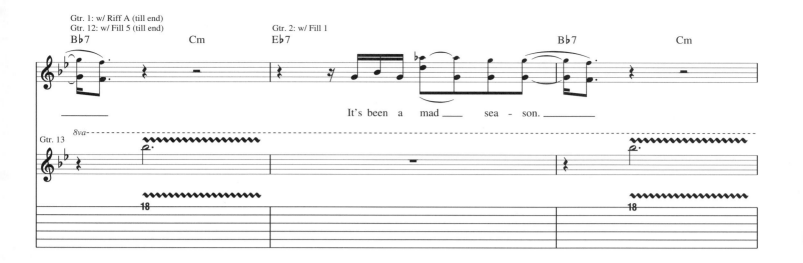

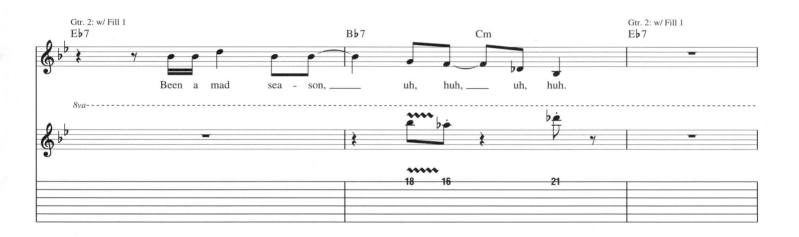

*Set an octave below.

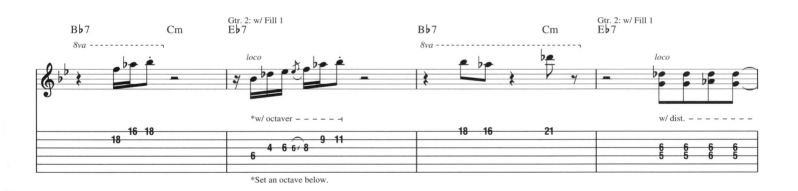

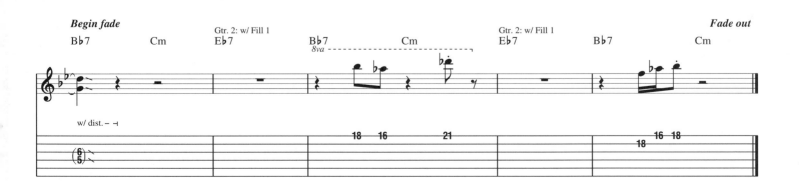

Rest Stop

Written by Rob Thomas

Gtr. 3: w/ Rhy. Fig. 4

The light was shin-ing from the ra - di - o, _____ and

I could bare-ly see ___ her face. ___ But she

Pre-Chorus
Gtr. 1: w/ Rhy. Fig. 2
Gtr. 2: w/ Fill 1

knew all the words _ that I nev-er had said, _ she knew the crum-pled up prom-ise of this bro-ken-down man. _ And as I

o - pened up the door, _____ she said,

65

Interlude

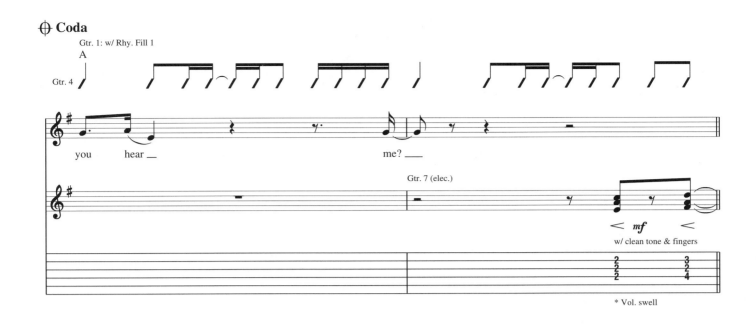

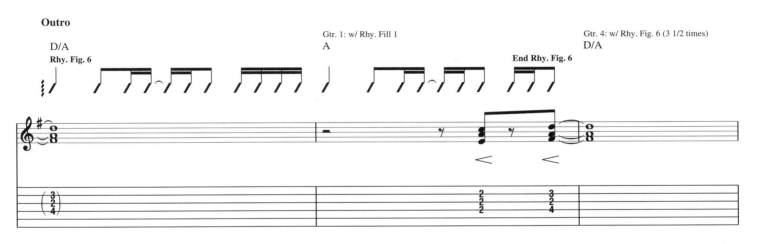

Outro

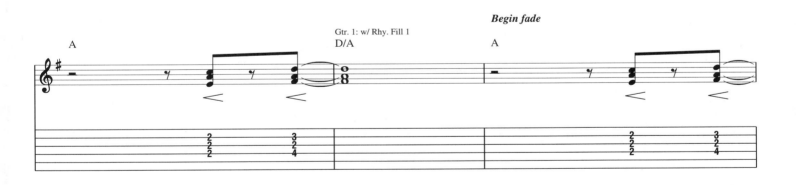

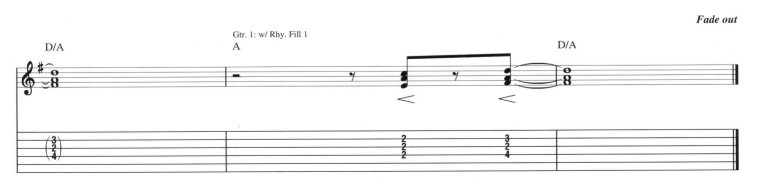

The Burn

Written by Rob Thomas

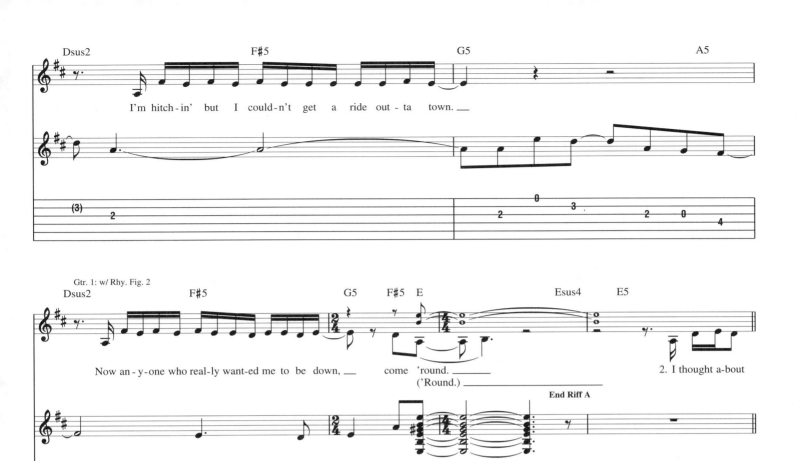

I'm hitch-in' but I could-n't get a ride out-ta town. ___

Now an-y-one who real-ly want-ed me to be down, ___ come 'round. ___
('Round.) ___
2. I thought a-bout

End Riff A

Gtr. 1: w/ Rhy. Fig. 2

Verse

Gtr. 1: w/ Rhy. Fig. 1 (2 times)   Gtr. 3: w/ Riff A

sing-in' but I could-n't re-mem-ber all of the words. ___
ev-'ry-thing and ev-'ry-one I need-ed be-fore. ___

Gtr. 2

Break-in' but I could-n't get the piec-es a-part. ___
Try'n' to get a han-dle on a rea-son to shine. ___

Gtr. 2

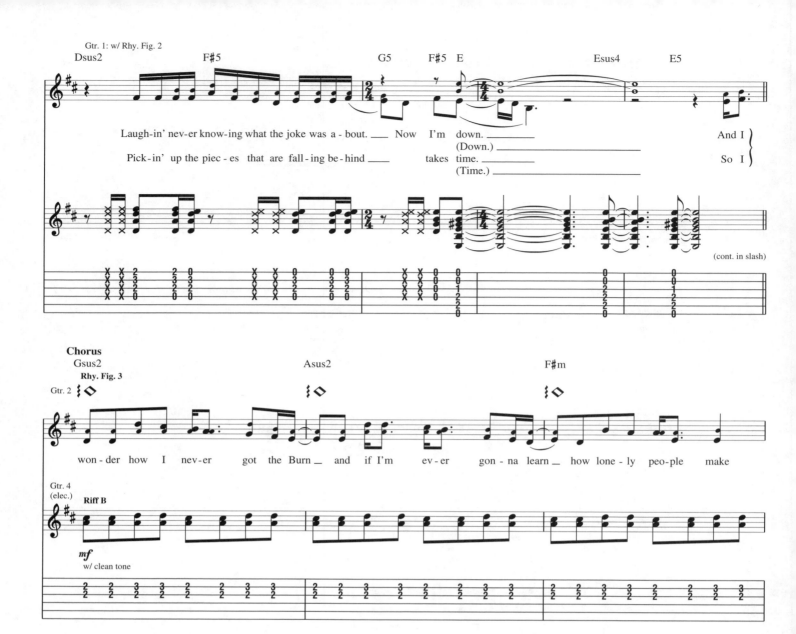

Laugh-in' nev-er know-ing what the joke was a-bout. ___ Now I'm down. ___ And I }
(Down.) _____
Pick-in' up the piec-es that are fall-ing be-hind ___ takes time. ___ So I }
(Time.) _____

(cont. in slash)

Chorus

won-der how I nev-er got the Burn ___ and if I'm ev-er gon-na learn ___ how lone-ly peo-ple make

w/ clean tone

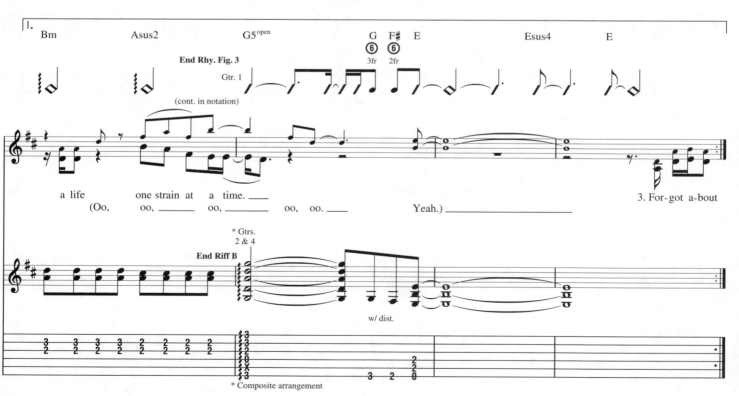

a life one strain at a time. ___
(Oo, oo, ___ oo, ___ oo, oo. ___ Yeah.) _____ 3. For-got a-bout

w/ dist.

* Composite arrangement

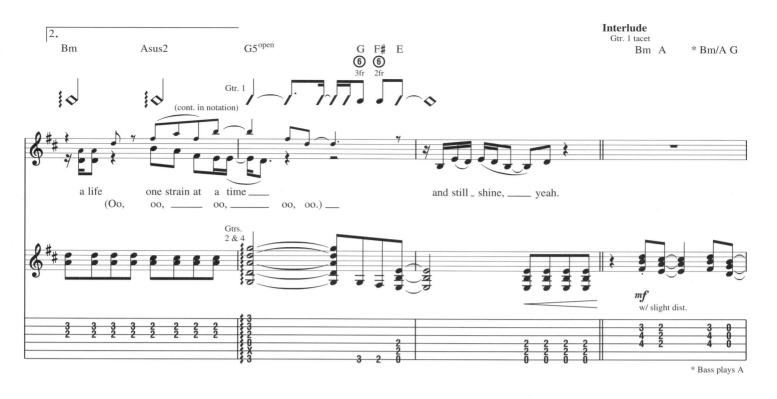

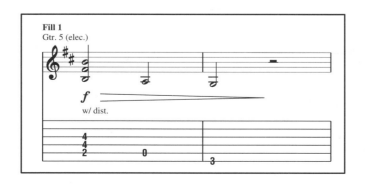

Chorus
Gtr. 2: w/ Rhy. Fig. 3 (2 times)
Gtr. 4: w/ Riff B (2 times)

won-der how I nev-er got the Burn __ and if I'm ev-er gon-na learn __ how lone-ly peo-ple make

a life. All this time I won-der how I nev-er got the Burn __ and if I'm ev-er gon-na learn __ how lone-ly peo-ple make

their life __ one strain at a time _____ and still shine. _____

(Oo.) _____
(Oo. _____ oo, _____ oo, oo.) __

Gtrs. 2 & 3

Bent

Written by Rob Thomas

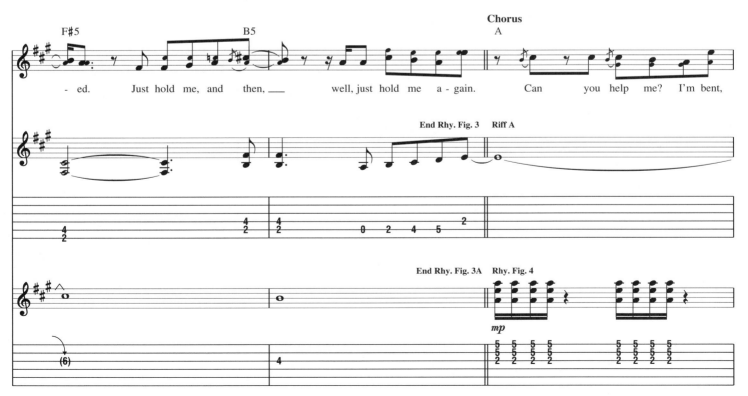

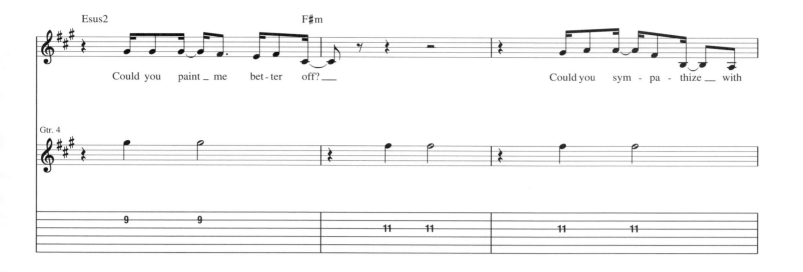

Could you paint _ me bet - ter off? ___   Could you sym - pa - thize _ with

Gtr. 4

Gtrs. 1 & 2: w/ Rhy. Figs. 3 & 3A

my needs? ___   I know you think _ I need _ a lot. ___   I start - ed out _ clean, but I'm jad -

𝄋 Chorus

1st time, Gtrs. 1 & 2: w/ Riff A & Rhy. Fig. 4
2nd time, Gtrs. 1 & 2: w/ Riff A & Rhy. Fig. 4 (1st 4 meas.)
3rd time, Gtrs. 1 & 2: w/ Riff A & Rhy. Fig. 4 (1st 6 meas.)

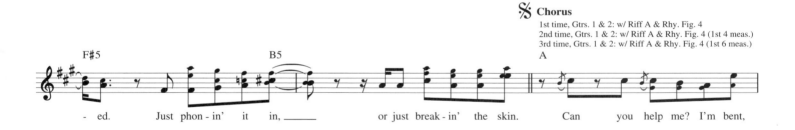

\- ed.   Just phon - in' it in, ___   or just break - in' the skin.   Can   you help me? I'm bent,

To Coda 1 ⊕

I'm so scared _ that I'll nev - er   get put back to - geth - er.   Keep break - in' me in

To Coda 2 ⊕

and this is how we will end: ___   with you and me ___   bent. ___
(How we will end.) ___

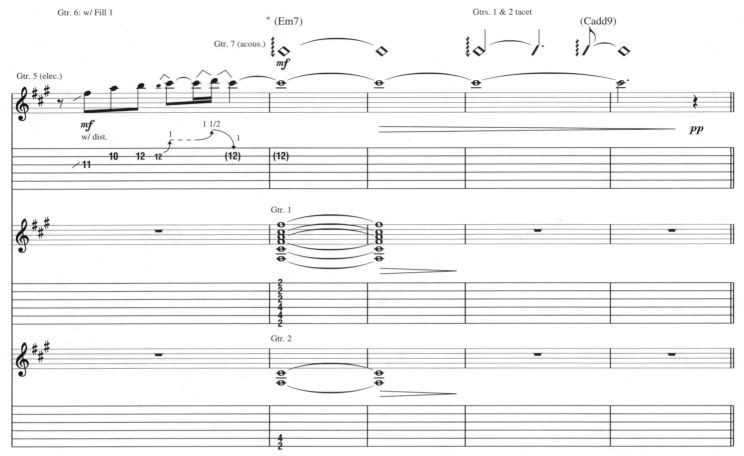

* Symbols in parentheses represent chord names respective to capoed guitar and do not reflect actual sounding chord.

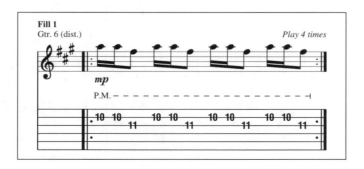

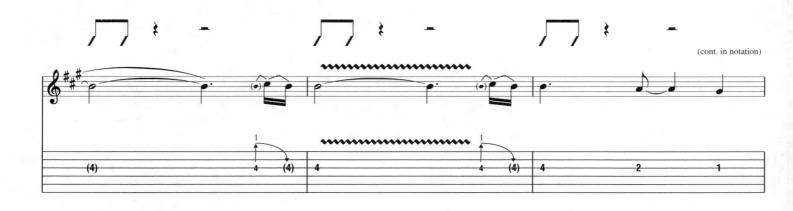

(cont. in notation)

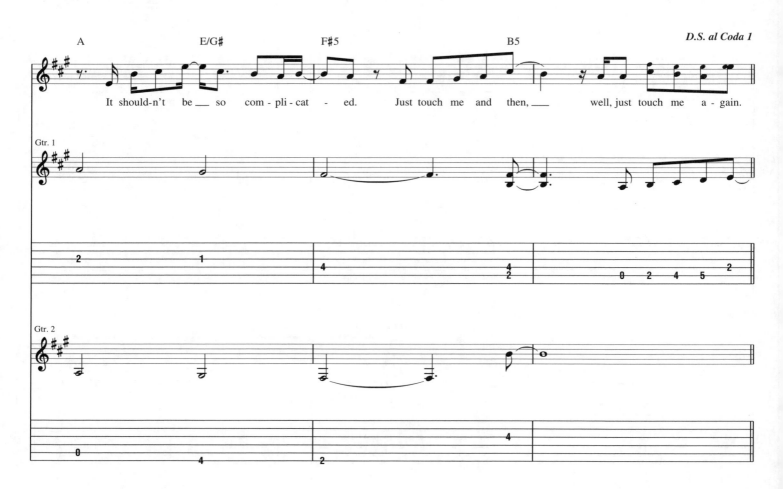

D.S. al Coda 1

A   E/G#   F#5   B5

It should-n't be __ so com-pli-cat - ed. Just touch me and then, __ well, just touch me a - gain.

Gtr. 1

Gtr. 2

◇ **Coda 1**

Gtrs. 1 & 2: w/ Riff A & Rhy. Fig. 4 (1st 4 meas.)

A   F#m7

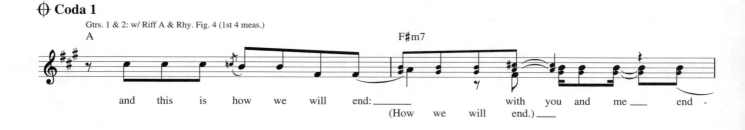

and this is how we will end: __ with you and me __ end-
(How we will end.) __

Dsus2   E   D.S. al Coda 2

- ing with - out __ un - der - stand - ing. Hell, I'll go there a - gain.

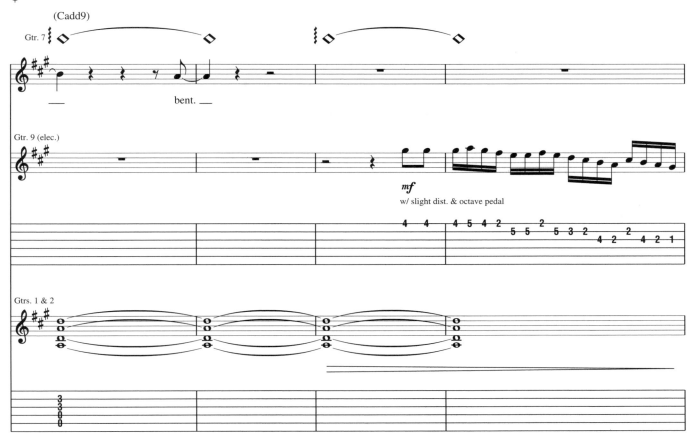

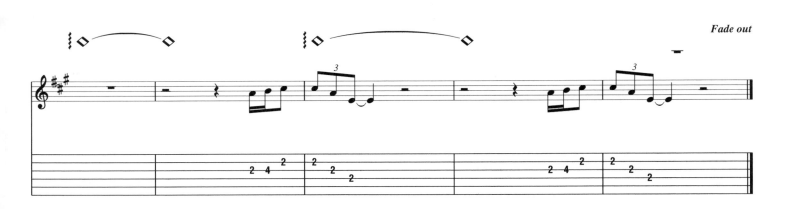

Bed of Lies

Written by Rob Thomas and Matt Serletic

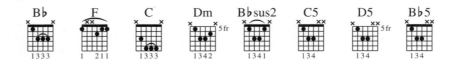

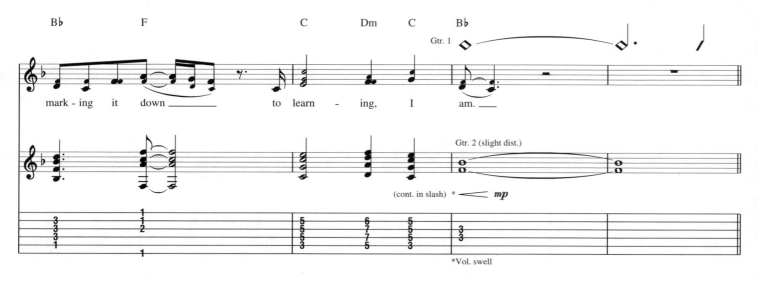

Verse

Gtr. 2 tacet

1. I don't think that I could take an-oth-er emp-ty mom-ent.
2. Don't wan-na be the one who turns the whole thing o-ver.

Gtr. 3 (slight dist.)

mp   P.M.   simile on repeats

I don't think that I could fake an-oth-er hol-low smile.
I don't wan-na be some-where where I just don't be-long,

Rhy. Fill 1   End Rhy. Fill 1

Well, it's not e-nough just to be lone-ly.
where it's not e-nough just to be sor-ry.

Gtr. 3

Gtr. 4 (dist.)

mp

Pre-Chorus
Gtr. 1: w/ Rhy. Fill 1
Gtr. 3 tacet

And just like me you've got needs ___ and they're on - ly ___ a ___
I tried to be more than me ___ and I gave ___ un - til ___ it

whis - per ___ a - way. ___ And we soft - ly sur - ren - der to these lives ___
all went ___ a - way. ___ And we've on - ly sur - ren - dered to the worst ___

let ring throughout

(cont. in slash)

86

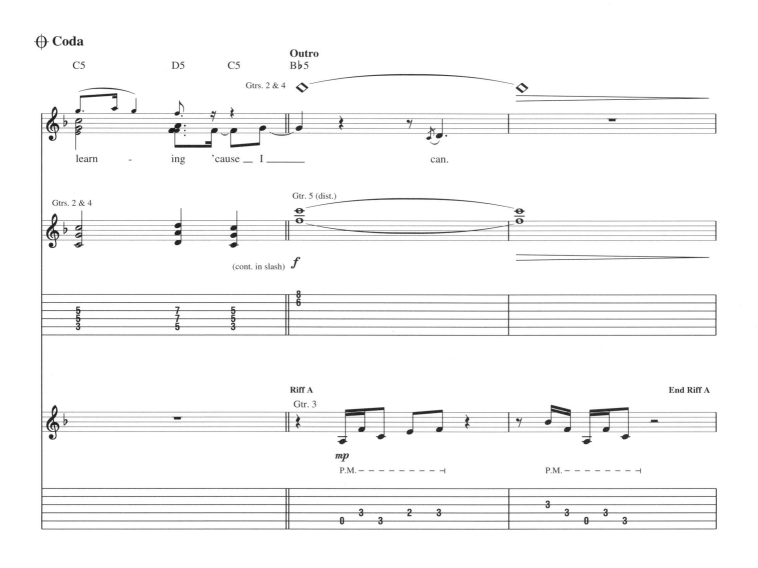

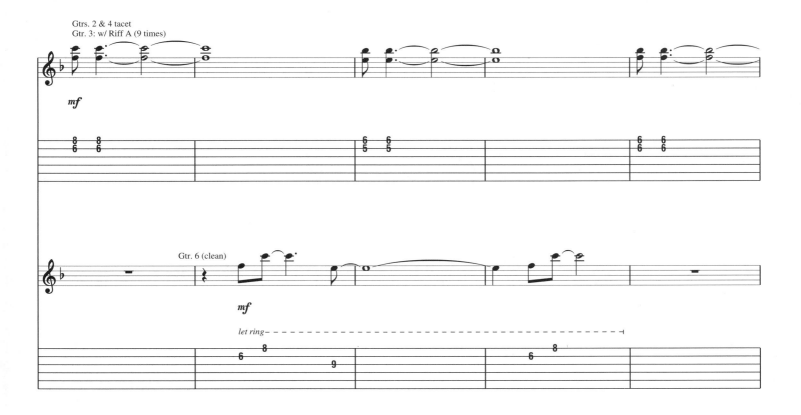

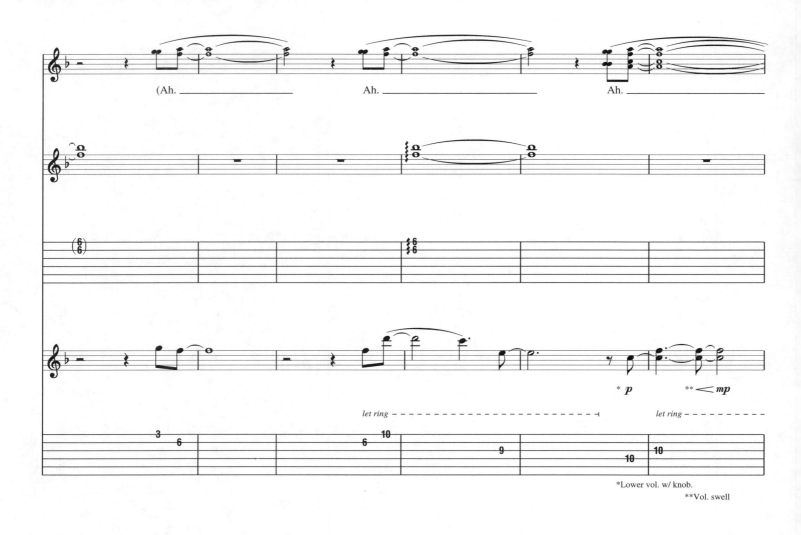

*Lower vol. w/ knob.
**Vol. swell

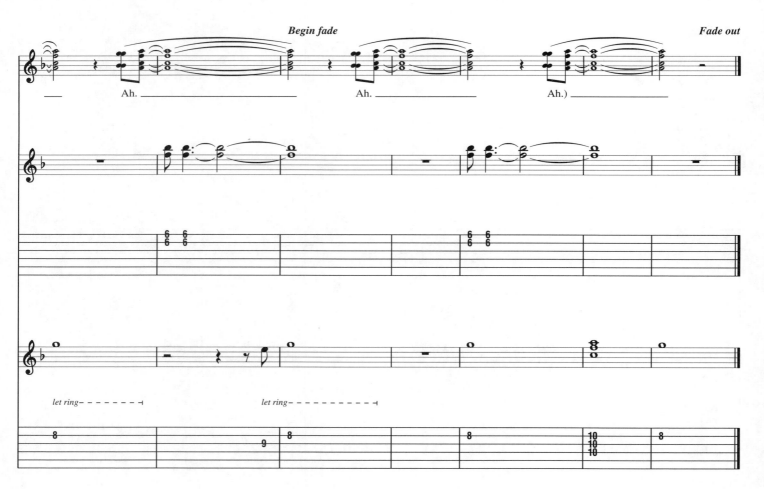

Leave

Written by Rob Thomas

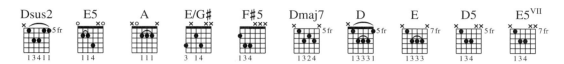

Gtrs. 3 & 4; Drop D tuning:
(low to high) D–A–D–G–B–E

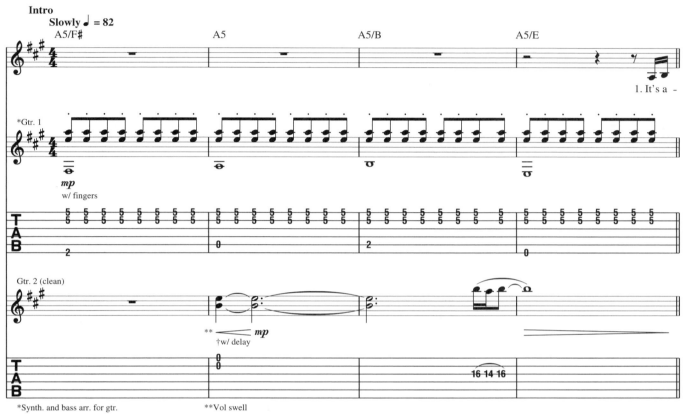

*Synth. and bass arr. for gtr.   **Vol swell

†Set for quarter note regeneration w/ 2 repeats.

*Chord symbols reflect implied harmony

how I turn __ my head __ and lose _____ it all. __ It's __ un-nerv-

Gtr. 2

delay off

p *

14 16
14/16   14
14
16
14
12

End Riff A

*Vol. swell

Gtr. 3: w/ Riff A

- ing   how just one __ move puts me   by my   - self. __   There you go __ just trust-ing   some -

Gtr. 2

mp

w/ delay

14
14 16

(14)
(12)

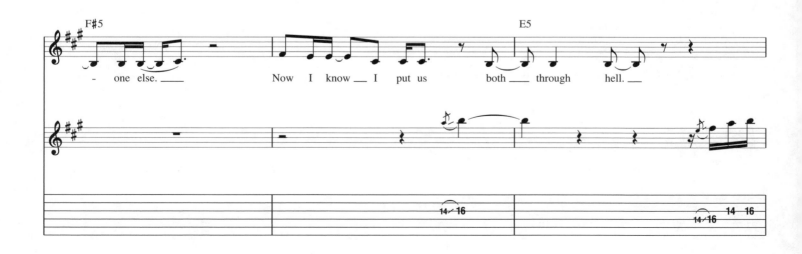

- one else. ____   Now   I   know __ I   put us   both ___ through   hell. __

14/16   14 16
14/16

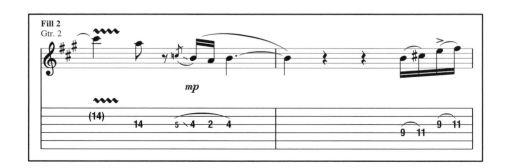

now, no, ___ no, the one ___ you're leav-ing out. ___
Ah. _____   Ah.) _____

Pre-Chorus
Gtrs. 2 & 5 tacet
Dsus2   E

I'm not say - ing   there was noth-ing   wrong, ___

*Gtr. 6

mp
w/ fingers

*Horns and bass arr. for gtr.

A   E5/B   F#m

I did - n't think you'd ev - er get   tired ___ of me. ___   But if that's   how you're gon - na leave, ___

Gtr. 2

hold bend

Gtr. 6

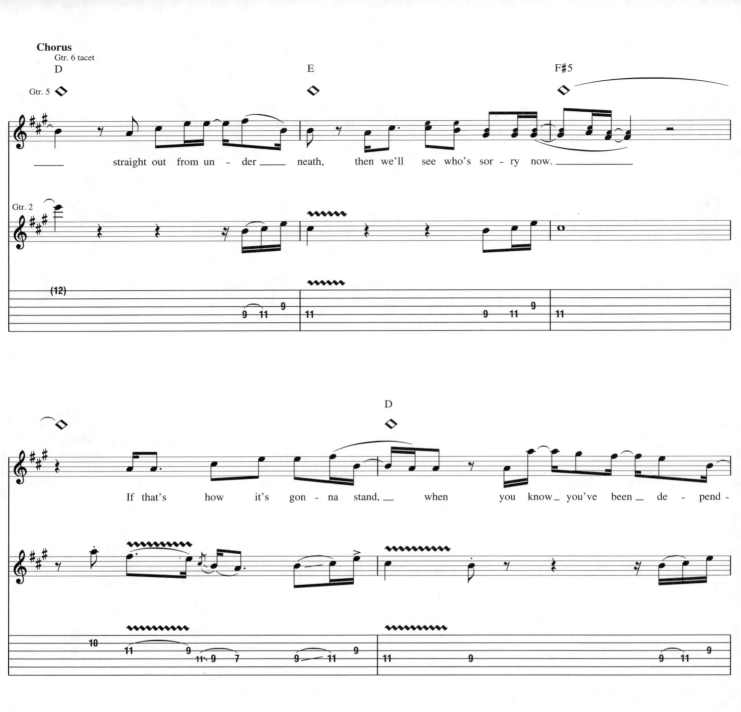

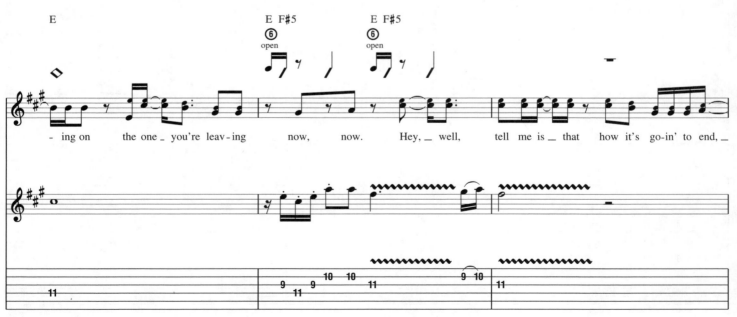

I'm the one _ you're leav-ing _____ now, _____ now, the one _ you're leav-ing out. _

Ah. _____

Ah). _____

Stop

Written by Rob Thomas and Paul Doucette

Gtrs. 1 & 3; Open E tuning:
(low to high) E–B–E–G#–B–E
Gtr. 5; Drop D tuning:
(low to high) D–A–D–G–B–E

Intro

Moderate Rock ♩ = 108

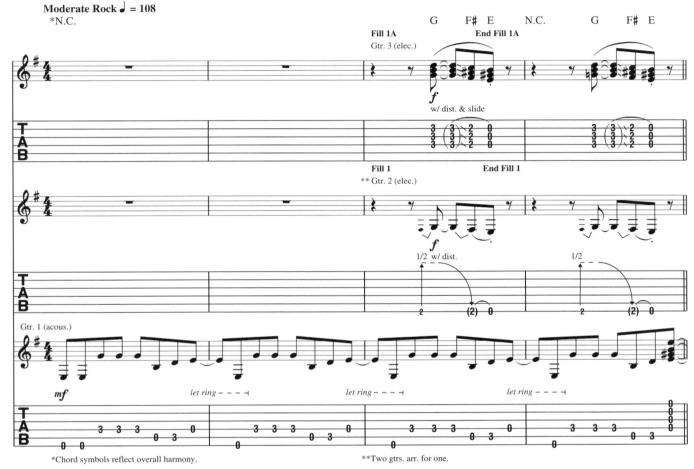

*Chord symbols reflect overall harmony.

**Two gtrs. arr. for one.

Verse

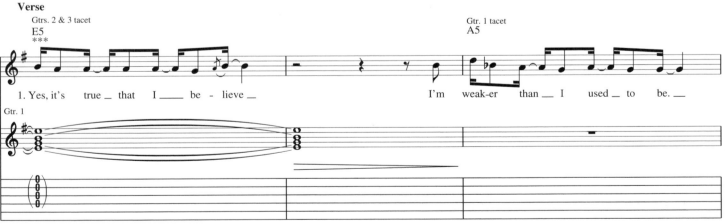

***Voc. doubled an octave lower (next 7 meas.)

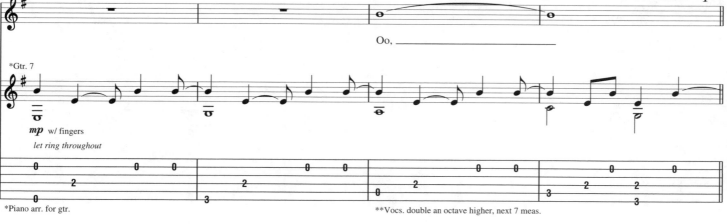

⊕ Coda

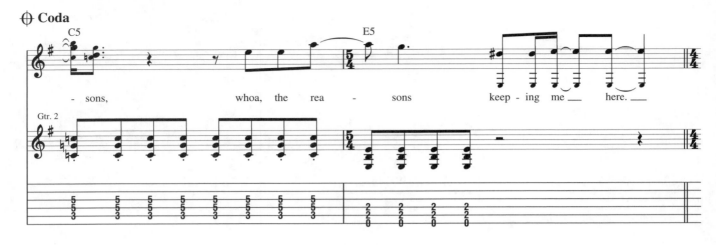

-sons,   whoa, the rea - sons   keep-ing me ___ here. ___

Interlude

w/ad lib Bkgd. Voc. till end
Gtr. 2 tacet
N.C.

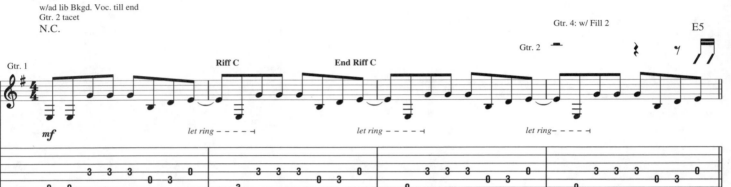

Outro

Gtr. 1: w/ Riff C (11 times)
Gtr. 8: w/ Rhy. Fig. 2 (13 times)
E5 type2

1st time, Bkgd. voc: w/ Voc. Fig. 1
2nd time, Gtr. 4: w/ Fill 2

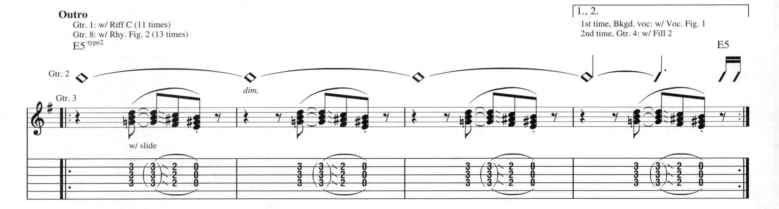

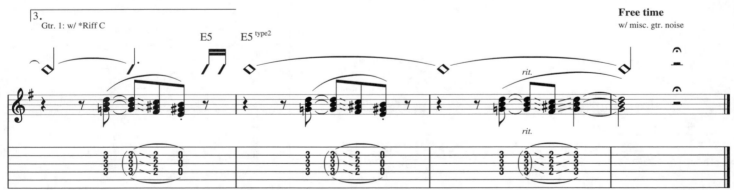

*Last note is not tied.

(You'll find what you think ain't gon-na be   true.) ___

106

You Won't Be Mine

Written by Rob Thomas

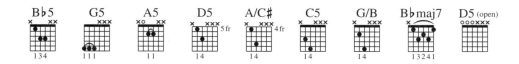

Gtr. 3; Drop D tuning:
(low to high) D–A–D–G–B–E

Intro
Slowly ♩ = 66

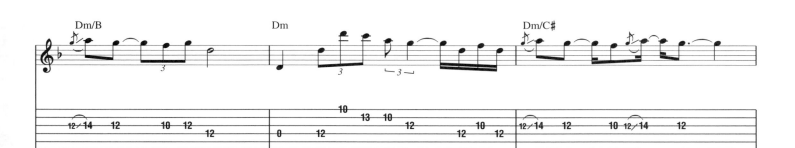

* Piano arr. for gtr.   ** Chord symbols reflect implied harmony.

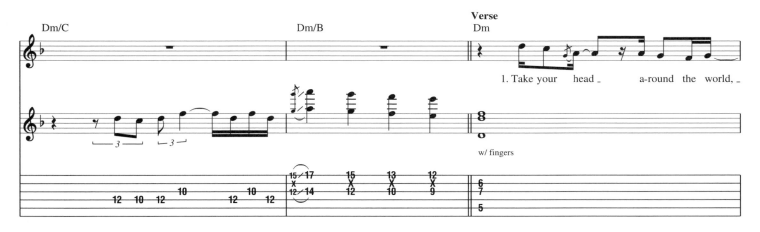

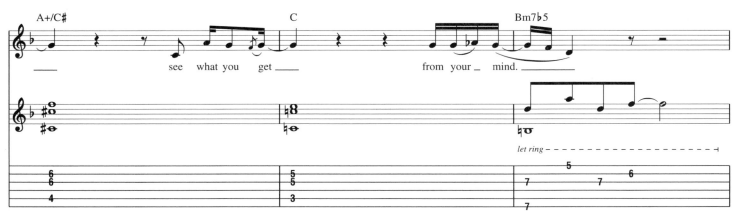

Write your soul down word for word, _ see who's your friend _ and who is kind. ____

Pre-Chorus

Well, it's al-most like _ a dis-ease, _____ and I know soon _ you will _
It's al-most like _ be-ing free, _____ yeah, well, I know soon _ you will _

* 2nd time, played ***p***

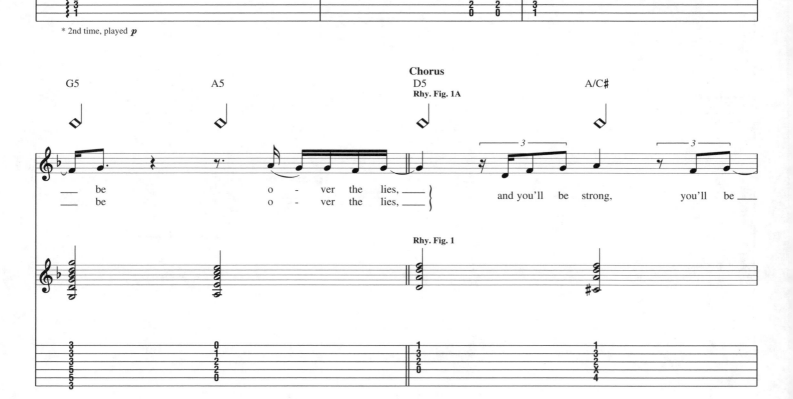

Chorus

_ be o - ver the lies, _____ and you'll be strong, you'll be _
_ be o - ver the lies, _____

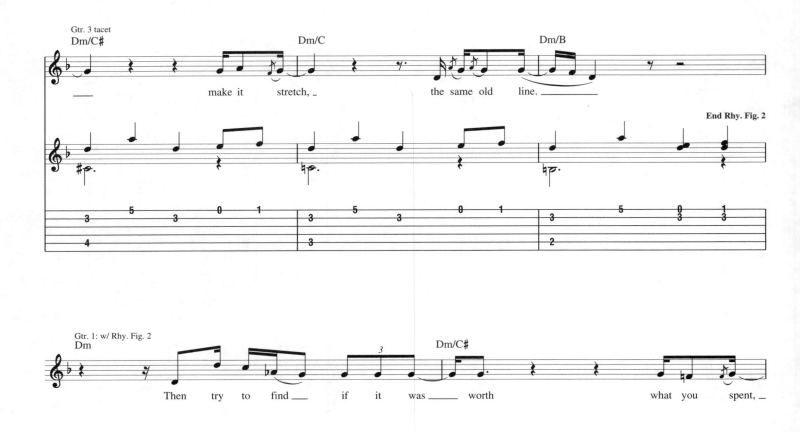

make it stretch, _ the same old line. _____

Then try to find ___ if it was ___ worth what you spent, _

why you're guilt - y for ___ the way ___ you're feel - ing now. _

D.S. al Coda

Coda

3. Well, take your - self _ out _____ to the curb, _

sit and _ wait, a fool _ for life. _ And it's al-most like _ a dis-ease. _

Well, I know soon _ you will _ be, you'll _ be o - ver the lies, _

Chorus

Gtrs. 1 & 2 tacet

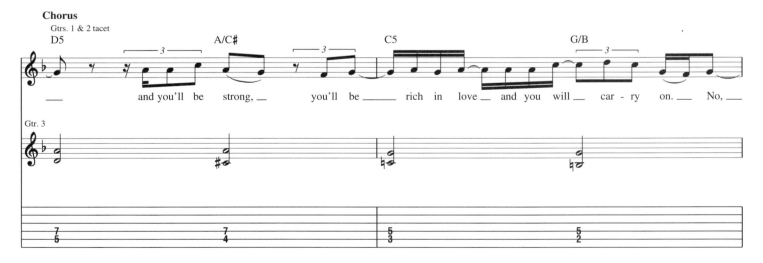

_ and you'll be strong, _ you'll be _____ rich in love and you will _ car - ry on. _ No, _